lake light

dave butcher

foreword by Joe Cornish

thanks

Thanks to my wife Jan for her unwavering support through the years. She has to work very hard keeping me organised, driving me everywhere to save my bad back and has taken over the booking for all of my photo trips as this wasn't my strong point!

Thanks to Joe Cornish, whose landscape photography I have admired for many years, for writing a foreword for Lake Light.

Thanks to Steven Brierley, and his colleagues at Harman Technology, for their continued support. In addition, Steven lives in the Lake District and offered invaluable advice and opened a few doors that I may not have found on my own.

Thanks to Andy Oakey and the rest of the folks at 10th Planet, Sheffield for the new design to my latest book and pulling everything together so quickly to keep us on schedule.

prints and further information

Prints of the photographs in Lake Light, and many other places, as well as further information are available from my business web site www.davebutcher.co.uk

peak light
dave butcher

Published in the UK by
Dave Butcher Photography
Briarwood,
Tunstead Milton,
Whaley Bridge,
High Peak,
Derbyshire,
SK23 7ER
www.davebutcher.co.uk

©2010 Dave Butcher Photography.
The images and text in this book are the copyright of Dave Butcher who asserts his moral rights to be identified as the author of the work. Copyright 2010.

British Library Cataloguing-in-Publication Data:
A catalogue record for this book is available from the British Library.

ISBN: 978-0-9555627-1-6
First edition 2010

Design and editorial production by 10th Planet.

Printed by South Yorkshire Printers.

contents

foreword by Joe Cornish

The geological origin of the Lake District is turbulent, volcanic, ancient. Multiple glacial cycles, and the high-energy weathering associated with its westerly maritime position have sculpted England's most dramatic and mountainous landscape. Some might say, England's only mountainous landscape. The fell tops may appear similar to the Scottish Highlands, but the valleys that divide them remind us that this region is quintessentially English. Once heavily mined and quarried for its mineral wealth, it is now occupied by a bucolic combination of hill farms, pretty villages, holiday homes and exceptional native woodland. The Lake District defines our idea of the picturesque.

It is largely this unique scenic appeal that makes the Lakes an outstandingly popular destination. This popularity is good for business. People come, looking, looking, quite literally, by the million (fifteen million or so in a typical year). So employment and prosperity flows directly from the beauty of the landscape. Many people in such a restricted space with relatively few roads can cause its own problems; traffic jams in the towns, and on the main routes between them are a serious problem in holiday periods. Yet in that immutable law of the great outdoors, as soon as the visitor sheds the cocoon of the car and moves more than five hundred metres from the car park onto the hill, the crowds melt away.

I have been visiting the Lake District for three decades, and realise I still know it only superficially. Its tortuous geology gives rise to great complexity and variety. A myriad of paths and routes make for pleasant walking, and to find every path and every view here would be the work of a lifetime. As well as a lot of paths it has an abundance of weather. The floods that devastated Cockermouth and Workington in November 2009 were exceptional, but local Cumbrians bore the disaster with characteristic stoicism and good humour. After all, they are a great deal more used to rain than most of us; the lakes do not fill the region's valleys by accident.

Like poets and artists of earlier generations, photographers are inevitably drawn here by the outstanding scenery. Yet the weather can make the task of taking pictures challenging. The best photographers are able to ride the challenge, to have patience, and to take advantage of the region's elusive light. Although it has a wealth of colour, this is a landscape that lends itself to black and white photography, as Dave Butcher's images so eloquently illustrate. Light and shade expressed in the silvery greyscale of a black and white photograph unifies the land and the sky, bringing harmony to disparate colours and textures. Looking at a great black and white photograph of the Lake District conveys a sense of timelessness and distillation, as if these are all the tones we need for a real understanding.

Of course, there is more to black and white photography than merely taking out the colour. Years of experience are required to develop the vision that recognises the most effective tonal relationships, and a sense of design, of balance, rhythm, energy and light are, if anything, even more critical than in colour photography. Dave Butcher remains a committed film photographer, and a genuine expert of traditional darkroom processes. Today there are a hundred different ways to arrive at a black and white print via the digital workflow. Yet if it ain't broke, why fix it? The quality of an outstanding silver gelatine print is still a unique photographic experience.

This devotion to classical methods has served him well. Using simple, high quality medium format cameras, he is undistracted by technical concerns and is able to focus all his attention on the light and the landscape, and to continue a process of documentation and interpretation he began many years ago.

As we enjoy this Lake District portfolio we realise that this is an exceptionally fit and agile photographer for whom long walks and high exposed summits and ridges are the stuff of life. Dave Butcher is a man truly at home in the landscape, whose pictures speak of a real personal connection with nature. I can think of no better way to be.

Joe Cornish

introduction

For this, my third book, the subject had to be the Lake District. A place I have spent many enjoyable days and weeks over the years, accompanied from the start, in the early 1970's, by the guide books of Alfred Wainwright and Ordnance Survey Tourist maps which I bought as needed, or as I could afford them.

Along with the Peak District, this was where I learnt to safely walk the hills while working for Unilever Research as a lab technician at the Frythe laboratories in Welwyn in the early 1970's. There were lots of camping trips, memorable visits to pubs, my first backpacking trip in 1972 (2 days around Eskdale and Wasdale) and a memorable crossing of the Lakes as part of Wainwright's coast-to-coast walk in 1978, the year I moved on from Unilever to do a PhD at Cambridge.

The book is somewhat arbitrarily divided into 3 sections and has a circular arrangement of pictures, starting in the north, going down the west side and finishing with the south and east.

Each section includes one of the three large mountains, Skiddaw, Scafell Pike and Helvellyn and other than that they fit around the photographs that I wanted to include here.

I have worked exclusively in black and white for over 10 years, a legacy of working for Ilford until 2002, manufacturer of the FP4 film and Multigrade papers that I use. For all of my photography I use medium format Mamiya film cameras and have done since 1986, in fact I sold my Nikon 35mm camera equipment in the early 1990's to buy a lens for my Mamiya 6 camera. Some technical details are included for each photograph in a table at the back of this book so you can see which camera and film was used and the date it was taken.

An article on the use of digital cameras for black and white landscape photography is included, since I know from the many courses that I run that this is what the majority of people now use. Most digital cameras have a number of unnecessary functions which can confuse to start with so I have tried to explain how to use those that will help most when taking landscapes in black and white. You can always learn how to use others once you understand the basics. If you are new to digital photography or would just like to progress, I hope it helps.

The majority of the book images (roughly three out of every four) were taken within the last 10 years but the oldest image dates back to a magical day on Striding Edge and Helvellyn in December 1984. We walked up through the clouds to clear blue skies above Striding Edge being mesmerised by seeing, for the first time, Brocken Spectres (shadows on clouds below) and Glories (circular rainbow around the Brocken Spectre) displayed all morning. A real day to remember!

The images used for this book are from scans of prints or negatives and they are then edited in Photoshop CS3 to roughly match what a darkroom print would look like. Each image has a detailed caption to help you visit the location and even find my tripod holes if you are a photographer. A map with the location of each photograph has also been included to assist you in this aim.

Selecting the images was enjoyable but not an easy task. The final set was chosen from a short list of over 200. If your favourite view didn't make it into this book maybe it will be in volume 2! Quite a few of the images which did not make it into the book are now on my web site www.davebutcher.co.uk so have a look here too.

During the 2 years leading up to the publication of this book my wife Jan and I made several trips to the Lakes and had lots of mixed weather, which always makes for interesting and dramatic lighting. A few blue sky days are always welcome but there is nothing like changeable weather to make for striking black and white photographs. There is usually a pub to retire to if the rain or snow becomes unbearable or seems to be set in for a few hours!

The book project also took us to some previously unvisited parts of the Lake District. I must admit to having a bias towards the high mountains but after all of these years it was still able to produce a few surprises on the coast and lower hills. A number of these are included in Lake Light and I hope you enjoy seeing the photographs as much as I enjoyed taking them and producing the images for this book.

Dave Butcher, December 2009

map

COCKERMOUTH

PENRITH

● Bassenthwaite
Plates: 21, 22

● Blencathra
Sharp Edge
Plate 6

KESWICK

Keswick Plates: 5, 10, 13 ●

● Castlerigg Stone Circle
Plates: 1, 3, 23, 61, 64

● Friars Crag
Plate 17

● High Rigg Plate 4, 87

● Aira Force
Plates: 57, 84

Whiteside
Plate 20 ●

● Wandope
Plates: 15, 19

● Ashness Bridge Plates: 2, 16

ULLSWATER

● South Derwent Water Plate 24

Scales Force
Plates: 48, 51 ●

● Crummock Water
Plate 12, 86

● Dalt Wood Plate 14

● Birkhouse Moor Plate 62

● Buttermere
Plates: 7, 8, 9, 11, 18, 25

● Watendlath
Plate 26

● Helvellyn Plates: 69, 74, 77

Ennerdale
Plate 32 ●

● Red Pike
Plate 29

● Birk Side Plate 79

● Raise Beck Plate 85

Scoat Fell Plate 54 ●

● High Street Plate 70, 82

Red Pike Plate 28 ●

● Wasdale Falls
Plates: 30, 49, 52

● Nan Bield Pass Plate 78

● Sprinkling Tarn
Plate 27

● Langdales
Plates: 37,
38, 39, 81

● Ill Bell Plate 63

Seatallan
Plate 52 ●

● Wast Water
Plate 44

● Rydal Grasmere Plates: 56, 66, 67

Wasdale
Plates: 30, 49 ●

● Ill Gill Head
Plate 55

● Upper Eskdale
Plate 42

● Loughrigg Fell Plates: 65, 72

● Esk Falls
Plates: introduction, 33, 35, 45, 46

● Elter Water
Plate 41

AMBLESIDE

● Hard Knott
Plates: 31, 47

SEASCALE

● Tarn Hows
Plate 76

WINDERMERE

CONISTON

● Wise Ean Tarn
Plate 73

Ravenglass
Plate 43 ●

● Devoke Water
Plate 36

● Coniston
Plate 71

● Brant Fell
Plate 80

● Walberthwaite
Plate 40

KENDAL

● Plain Riggs
Plate 59, 60

Eskmeals
Plate 34 ●

● Scout Scar
Plate foreword, 75

● Gummer How
Plate 83

● Raven Barrow
Plates: 58, 68

MILNTHORPE

▶

1. Blencathra from Castlerigg Stone Circle

The standing stones of Castlerigg stone circle
make good foregrounds with Blencathra in
the background. Close to Keswick.

10

section 1
the northern lake district

The main town in this area is Keswick, a bustling small town, on the edge of Derwent Water, with lots going on. Immediately to the north is Skiddaw, the largest mountain in this area at 931m, 3054 feet and the third highest in England after Scafell Pike and Helvellyn, but just the 6th highest top.

Other notable features are Castlerigg Stone Circle with clear views of Skiddaw, Blencathra and the Helvellyn range. Bassenthwaite Lake with Skiddaw behind was an interesting place, as I was setting up for a shot someone approached and seeing my camera on a tripod asked if I was photographing the Ospreys; I didn't know until then that the area is a stronghold for Ospreys in England.

Watendlath Tarn above the picturesque Borrowdale was a very tranquil place, unlike the busy Ashness Bridge which you pass on the way. For some of the best hill walking in the Lake District there are also the mountains of Blencathra, Grisedale Pike, Grasmoor, Robinson and Dale Head.

Of the lower viewpoints in this area Cat Bells (451m, 1480 feet) may not be the highest peak but it has a spectacular position overlooking Derwent Water and Keswick. It was also made famous by Beatrix Potter as the home of 'Mrs Tiggywinkle'. Cat Bells is best seen from Friars Crag (a small rocky promontory) across Derwent Water near Keswick.

Buttermere is also included in this section, one of the most photogenic places in the whole of the Lake District. There are two lakes, Buttermere and Crummock Water, surrounded by big mountains. The village itself has 2 hotels and a few other places to stay. It is a fantastic base for hill walking as well as photography of lakes, mountains, streams, waterfalls and shapely trees. It is also a stronghold for Red Squirrels, now quite rare in England.

2. Ashness Bridge

The old packhorse bridge on the road to Watendlath. The stream is Barrow Beck which runs down from High Seat into Derwent Water. A snow-capped Skiddaw is in the background.

3. Blencathra from Castlerigg Stone Circle, Infra-red
Taken at the same time as plate 1 on Ilford infra-red film to darken the sky and lighten the sunlit foliage.

4. Blencathra from High Rigg

At 343 m this is not a high viewpoint but it has uninterrupted views of Blencathra, Skiddaw and Helvellyn.

5. Blencathra and Keswick
A snow-capped Blencathra and Keswick church spire from Crow Park beside Derwent Water

6. Blencathra Sharp Edge
Sharp Edge as seen from the flank of Blencathra

7. Winter Sun, Buttermere
The frozen and snow covered Buttermere lake on a frosty morning with Fleetwith Pike on the left, Haystacks behind the main tree and High Crag on the right.

8. Buttermere and Fleetwith Pike #1
A small Silver Birch tree beside a partially frozen and snow-covered Buttermere lake.

9. Buttermere Tree Reflections Tree reflections in Buttermere lake with Robinson Crag in the background.

10. Cat Bells and Derwent Water from Crow Park Keswick Derwent Isle in Derwent water with Cat Bells behind, Causey Pike on the right.

11. Buttermere and Fleetwith Pike #3 The same tree as in Plate 8 but 8 years later. Quite a few branches have gone and Buttermere lake is swollen by heavy rain to cover the tree roots.

12. Crummock Water and Mellbreak Reflections

Reflections of Mellbreak and a fence in Crummock Water from near Wood House.

13. Causey Pike and Grisedale Pike from Derwent Water

Snow-capped Causey Pike (left) and Grisedale Pike (right) from Derwent Water landing stages at Keswick. The old jetty posts caught my eye and I was careful to put them against the hillside and not the sky.

15. Grasmoor from Wandope
Easy hill walking mixed with impressive ridges on the Grasmoor range.

16. Derwent Water and Skiddaw from Surprise View
Surprise View is on the road to Watendlath, above Ashness Bridge, and is a great viewpoint.

17. Cat Bells from Friars Crag
The Jaws of Borrowdale on the left and a snowy Cat Bells on the right.

14. Dalt Wood Borrowdale
Trees and lichen-covered rocks between Grange and Rosthwaite

18. Buttermere Reflections and Fleetwith Pike
Reflections in Buttermere lake with Fleetwith Pike on the right from the southeast end of the lake.

19. Sail, Ard Crags and Helvellyn from Wandope

Sail (left), Ard Crags (centre) and Helvellyn (background) from Wandope. The shadows of the clouds on the hill sides make the shot for me.

20. Mellbreak and Crummock Water from Whiteside
Infra-red film darkened the lake and lightened the hillsides, across the valley and beyond, from Whiteside near Grasmoor and above the village of Buttermere

21. Skiddaw, Bassenthwiate and Log

Ilford infra-red film was used to darken and add contrast to the sky. It also brightened the sunlit trees and grasses.

22. Skiddaw and Bassenthwaite
Skiddaw in the centre background with Ullock Pike on the left from the shore of Bassenthwaite Lake near Keswick

23. Skiddaw from Castlerigg Stone Circle
The viewpoint was chosen to avoid people appearing in the picture. The large stone on the left gives the image a strong foreground

24. Skiddaw and Derwent Water
Skiddaw and Derwent Water from the south end of the lake near Grange

25. Buttermere Icy Shoreline
Frosted trees, ice along the shore and reflections in
Buttermere lake.

26. Watendlath Tarn
The view across Watendlath Tarn to the High Seat
hills dusted with snow.

▶

27. Great Gable from Sprinkling Tarn
A short distance from Esk Hause this view over
Sprinkling Tarn provides a great reflection in
less than perfect conditions.

section 2
the western lake district

For this book the Western Lakes includes the mountains just south of Buttermere down to Wrynose and the Duddon Valley, and across to the Langdales with the lakes of Ennerdale Water, Wast Water and Elter water. Quite a small area but lots packed in for the hiker and photographer.

There are no towns comparable in size to Keswick, just villages and hamlets like Ennerdale Bridge, Wasdale Head, Santon Bridge, Boot and Elterwater.

This area has the highest and most rugged mountains in England with Scafell Pike being the highest at 978m, 3209 feet. It is surrounded by large peaks such as Scafell and Great Gable and is most easily seen from the road in Wasdale.

On the north side of Wasdale is the shapely peak of Yewbarrow and the peaks to the south of Ennerdale, including Pillar and Scoat Fell. To the north of Ennerdale is a narrow line of peaks with Buttermere on the far side. This is ridge walking country and includes Red Pike, High Stile, High Crag and Haystacks. This last peak was the favourite mountain of Alfred Wainwright, the author of the classic Lakeland walking guides.

South of the Scafell range is Eskdale with the village of Boot. This is a good base that is also close to the lakes, mountains and streams of Wasdale, the Duddon Valley and the coast at Ravenglass. A 1-in-3 single track road leads east to the Hardknott Pass with good views from the road and even better after climbing a few hundred yards above the road for clear views to the Scafell range and the Old Man of Coniston, with Bowfell and Crinkle Crags just to the east.

Farther east are the Langdale Pikes, including Harrison Stickle and Pavey Ark, which provided the single best day of Lake District winter walking I have ever had.

28. Great Gable and Scafell Range
Great Gable (left), Scafell Pike (right of cairn)
and Scafell (right) from the Wasdale Red Pike

29. Ennerdale Water from Red Pike
Ennerdale Water and the coast beyond from the
Buttermere Red Pike.

30. Yewbarrow, Great Gable and Wast Water
Yewbarrow (left), snow-capped Great Gable (centre background) and the flank of Scafell Pike (right) from Wast Water.

31. Bowfell and Crinkle Crags from Hard Knott
Bowfell (centre background) and Crinkle Crags (right) from Hard Knott above the Hardknott Pass.

32. Ennerdale Water
View to Steeple from the north shore of Ennerdale Water near Bowness.

34. Coast near Eskmeals
The beach and coast near Eskmeals and Bootle with Black Combe in the background shrouded in clouds. Just 4 miles south of Ravenglass

33. Esk Falls #2
The wide view of Esk Falls
Less than 2 miles northeast of
Brotherilkeld in Eskdale

36. Devoke Water
The view west across Devoke Water on Birker Fell above Eskdale.

35. Esk Falls #1
Esk Falls after heavy rain at the head of Eskdale near Brotherilkeld and Boot.

37. Pavey Ark and Stickle Tarn
Pavey Ark behind a frozen and snow covered Stickle Tarn in the Langdale Pikes.

38. Harrison Stickle
In the Langdale Pikes near Ambleside in Winter. Taken from near Stickle Tarn with Stickle Ghyll in the foreground.

39. Helvellyn range from Harrison Stickle
Helvellyn in full winter conditions from the summit of Harrison Stickle in the Langdale Pikes.

40. High Walberthwaite View
The view northeast over Yellow Flag Iris and Bull Rushes, near Ravenglass.

41. Langdale Pikes from Elter Water
A pair of Mute Swans on Elter Water. Harrison Stickle and Pavey Ark are the 2 main peaks in view.

42. Scafell Pike

Scafell Pike and the River Esk from Upper Eskdale near Great Moss. Scafell (left), Scafell Pike (right of the dip), Ill Crag (right). Taken on infra-red film to darken the sky and lighten the grasses below the rocks.

43. Ravenglass Boats

Boats on the River Esk estuary at Ravenglass with Black Combe on the right in the background

44. Scafell Pike from Wast Water Lingmell (left), Scafell Pike (centre) and Scafell (right) from Wast Water

40

45. Lingcove Falls Reflections
Reflections of the falls in summer. Upper Eskdale, less than 2 miles from Brotherilkeld.

47. Scafell Range from Hard Knott
View from Hard Knott to the Scafell range. Scafell left of centre,
Scafell Pike right of the large dip , then Broad Crag in the
background. Ill Crag on the right

◄

46. Lingcove Falls
The waterfall at the foot of Lingcove Beck,
after heavy rain. Near Esk Falls.

48. Scales Force #1
The lower in a series of waterfalls in a narrow ravine below Little Dodd. Less than 2 miles from Buttermere village.

49. Yewbarrow, Great Gable and Wast Water, Infra-red
Yewbarrow (left), Great Gable (centre at end of lake) and Wast Water. Taken on Ilford infra-red film to give the dramatic sky.

50. Wasdale Head Rapids
Rapids on Mosedale Beck behind the Wasdale Head Hotel, near the track to Black Sail Pass

51. Scales Force #3 Detail at the foot of the falls and Scales Beck, less than 2 miles from Buttermere. A slow shutter speed of 1 second of so at f22 gives the blurry effect to the water.

52. Seatallan Falls, Wasdale
A small waterfall on Greendale Gill on the lower slopes of Seatallan near Wasdale.

53. Wasdale Head Falls
Some waterfalls a few metres from the trail to Black Sail Pass from the Wasdale Head Hotel.

54. Scoat Fell View to Steeple and Ennerdale
Scoat Fell view to Steeple (with sun on it) and Ennerdale in the background

▶

**55. Yewbarrow and Wast Water
from Ill Gill Head**
Wasdale including Yewbarrow
(centre), Kirk Fell to the right in the
shadow, Pillar (left background)
and Wast Water from Ill Gill Head

▶

56. Rydal Water
Rydal Water in the morning from the woods at the
western end. Between Ambleside and Grasmere

section 3
the southern and eastern lake district

This is the largest area and covers several towns and large villages like Coniston, Windermere, Ambleside, Grasmere and Kendal. Being closest to the motorway it is also the easiest to reach.

There are lots of mountains including Helvellyn, second highest in England (third highest top), Fairfield, The Old Man of Coniston and the High Street range. Helvellyn also has the most famous narrow ridge in England, Striding Edge, as well as expansive views from the top in every direction across Lakeland.

Lakes include Coniston Water, Esthwaite Water, Windermere, Rydal Water, Grasmere, Thirlmere, Ullswater and Haweswater Reservoir in the east. Many of these are in spectacular positions and can be viewed, and photographed, from the shore as well as from high above. There are also many smaller lakes called tarns, such as Tarn Hows near Coniston and Wise Een Tarn near Sawrey.

This is the part of the Lake District with the most trees, especially in Grizedale Forest between Coniston and Windermere. It is easy walking country but the views can be restricted. This is also the centre of the Beatrix Potter attractions with several of her properties that provided the locations for many of her books.

The area between and south of Windermere and Kendal is more heavily farmed with rolling countryside and large limestone outcrops such as Scout Scar and Whitbarrow Scar providing great views and some contrast to the rest of Lakeland.

Further north is High Street, a wide flattish topped peak used by the Romans as a safer route rather than travelling through the wooded valleys below. This area is often a quieter part of the Lake District where you can get away from the crowds.

57. Aira Force
Aira Force waterfall with a packhorse bridge at the top and a narrow twisting ravine limiting the viewpoints for taking photographs. Near Glenridding and Ullswater.

58. Raven Barrow The view northeast from Raven Barrow on Cartmel Fell. About 4 miles northeast of Newby Bridge.

59. Old Man of Coniston and Dow Crag
Old Man of Coniston (right) and Dow Crag (left) from
Plain Riggs, about 1 mile south of Torver.

60. Old Man of Coniston and Tree
Old Man of Coniston (left of tree), Dow Crag (left of dip in background)
from the same location as used in plate 59.

61. Helvellyn from Castlerigg Stone Circle, Infra-red
Helvellyn in the background just left of the nearest standing stone. Taken on Ilford infra-red film to darken the sky and emphasise the shadows on the hillside. Compare with plate 64.

62. Helvellyn from Birkhouse Moor
Helvellyn (centre) from Birkhouse Moor above Patterdale, with Striding Edge on the left and Swirral Edge on the right

63. Helvellyn from Ill Bell
Helvellyn, in the background where the clouds dip down closest to the mountains, from the top of Ill Bell near Kentmere.

64. Helvellyn from Castlerigg Stone Circle
Helvellyn in the background just left of the nearest standing stone. Taken on Ilford FP4 film with a dark yellow filter to darken the sky and lighten the foliage. Compare with plate 61.

65. Grasmere from Loughrigg Fell
Grasmere lake, Grasmere village and Helm Crag centre background from Loughrigg Fell.

66. Grasmere Reflections #1

Morning reflections in Grasmere with Silver How in the background. Taken from the waters edge at the south end of the lake.

67. Grasmere Reflections #2

A slightly different view of the reflections in Grasmere. This time with Helm Crag in the centre background. Also taken from the south end of the lake, note the clouds more distinct in the reflection.

**68. Middle Tarn
Old Jetty**

An old, rotting and very
overgrown jetty in Middle
Tarn, near the track to
Raven's Barrow from Sow
How at the south end of
Lake Windermere.

69. Helvellyn from Striding Edge

Helvellyn summit from Striding Edge on a spectacular sunny day with fresh snow.

70.High Street Sky
A spectacular sky and a patchwork of snow on the hills. Taken from High Street looking northwest, near Kentmere

71. Old Man of Coniston and Coniston Water
The Old Man of Coniston (left background) with a yacht and kayak on Coniston Water, from the north end of the lake.

72. Rydal Water from Loughrigg Fell
The view across Rydal Water to Heron Pike (left) and both ends of the Fairfield horseshoe.

73. Wise Ean Tarn Sawrey
Wise Ean Tarn, in the heart of Beatrix Potter country, between Hawkshead and near Sawrey.
In the background are the Langdale Pikes on the right and the Coniston range in the centre.
Taken on a very wet day.

▶

74. Striding Edge in Winter
Striding Edge covered in fresh snow, taken
from the steep flank of Helvellyn

75. Scout Scar Edge
The edge of Scout Scar looking north with the north end of the Lyth Valley on the left. Also called Underbarrow Scar and just 2 miles west of Kendal.

76. Tarn Hows

Reflections in Tarn Hows, near Coniston, with the Langdale Pikes just visible in the Background. Once owned by Beatrix Potter, passed on to the National Trust.

77. Striding Edge and St Sunday Crag from Helvellyn
Striding Edge (left foreground) and St Sunday Crag (centre sunlit) from Helvellyn, with the High Street and Kentmere ridges in the background.

78. Small Water and Haweswater from Nan Bield Pass

The view from roughly half-way around the Kentmere Horseshoe. Looking down on Small Water with Haweswater Reservoir in the background. High Street is just out of shot on the left.

79. Thirlmere from Helvellyn
Thirlmere from the snow-covered flank of Helvellyn at Birk Side. Skiddaw is
hidden in the clouds background right.

80. Brant Fell View North

The view north from Brant Fell towards the Helvellyn range with Lake Windermere on the left.
The village of Bowness is less than a mile below to the left.

81. Windermere from the Langdales
The view along Great Langdale to Lake Windermere from Harrison Stickle in the Langdale Pikes. A frozen and snow-covered Stickle Tarn is in the left foreground.

82. Windermere from High Street
Lake Windermere from High Street in winter, near Thornthwaite Crag.
The ridge in the foreground leads to Froswick and Ill Bell.

83. Windermere from Gummer How
The view north over Lake Windermere from Gummer How just north of Newby Bridge with some windswept trees in the foreground.

84. Ullswater Trees
An old Silver Birch tree that has seen better days, with Ullswater behind. A snowy St Sunday Crag is the mountain in the centre background. About 2 miles north of Glenridding.

▶

85. Winter Thaw, Raise Beck
Partly frozen waterfall on Raise Beck above Dunmail Raise, north of Grasmere

using digital cameras for black and white landscape photography

Introduction

There are many types and manufacturers of digital cameras available so these notes refer to Nikon and Canon who make up the bulk of the camera market. If you have any other brand interpret the advice to suit your camera.

Camera settings before taking an image

Image Quality: RAW (NEF Nikon; CRW Canon)

Cameras use JPEG and RAW image file formats. If you intend to make large prints or edit your images use RAW. When you transfer images to your computer standardise on TIFF files for editing (either Convert to TIFF or use the Save As command). This will give the best image quality. After editing, convert back to JPEG when you save for web, this gives smaller file sizes.

Use Colour mode for easy image manipulation in your image editor. Some cameras will take a colour image and display on the camera screen in black and white.

Exposure

Exposure is made up of 3 basic settings, aperture, shutter speed and ISO sensitivity. They are all inter-related, as you change one it impacts on the others.

When using your camera's meter it will try and balance them out so, as you use a smaller aperture (large f-number like f22) it will automatically give you a slower shutter speed to make sure that the overall light level reaching the camera sensor is kept constant. You can over-ride these settings on all except the simplest cameras.

Changes in exposure are referred to in amounts called stops. A stop is a doubling or halving of the light used to make the image, depending on which way you make a change. It refers to the difference between settings not to the aperture, shutter speed or ISO numbers themselves.

This is reasonably straightforward for shutter speed and ISO sensitivity because normal numbers are involved, such as 1/30 to 1/60 or ISO 100 to ISO 200, each difference is 1 stop and the numbers have halved or doubled.

The aperture scale, on the other hand, has no obvious logic to the average photographer but has to be learned to allow you to take control of your exposures.

Aperture, commonly referred to as f-numbers

The scale used here is a little confusing to the newcomer to photography and it helps if you can remember a few numbers.

The f-stop range, where each number is one stop apart:

f2 - f2.8 – f4 – f5.6 – f8 – f11 – f16 – f22 – f32

More of the scene will be in focus at the larger numbers. This also means that less light will reach the camera sensor in a given time and consequently longer shutter times will be required to make an image.

For example, f22 will give images in focus from close to the lens to the far distance, whereas f4 will have much less in focus.

Shutter speed

Fast shutter speeds can stop action, such as 1/500 second, whereas slow shutter speeds will produce image blur in parts of an image that are moving, such as 1/15 second. If you want to adjust your exposure in stops using shutter speed then halving or doubling the number of your current exposure is 1 stop. To reduce a 1 second exposure by 1 stop use ½ second, for 2 stops use ¼ second.

ISO sensitivity setting

This used to be called film speed, now it just refers to the sensitivity of the digital camera sensor.

For general landscapes under good lighting use 100 ISO. For low light landscapes try ISO 400 or 800 but you will notice some drop in image quality.

The ISO scale works in a similar way to aperture and shutter speed. A doubling or halving of the value is a change of 1 stop. So from ISO 100 to 200 is 1 stop, 100 to 400 is 2 stops, etc. The lower the number, the less noise there will be in the images. The higher the number, the more noise there will be in an image but less light is needed to take an image and still keep detail.

In the absence of a tripod increase the ISO setting until the shutter speeds for the exposure you want to take are fast enough to hand hold.

86. Grasmoor and Crummock Water Grasmoor (left), Whiteless Pike (right) and Crummock Water

Mode: Aperture Priority – Av (Canon), A (Nikon)

This is the most useful setting for landscape photography. Mostly we are concerned with what is going to be in focus in the images that we take and this is exactly what the aperture controls.

Using a tripod will mean that when you are using a small aperture (e.g. f22), to bring more of the image into focus, you can still take the picture even though the shutter speed is too slow to hand hold without seeing camera blur.

Mode: Shutter Speed Priority – Tv (Canon), S (Nikon).

Mostly of use for action shots; for landscapes this would include moving water, fast moving skiers, etc. Fast shutter speeds of 1/125, 1/250 or 1/500 will all freeze the motion of water to varying amounts. Depending on the speed of the water that you are photographing you could see individual droplets frozen in space at these speeds.

For the streaky, almost dream-like, effect with water you need slow shutter speeds and a tripod. Usually somewhere in the region of ½ or ¼ second will give this effect. To achieve this you will need to close the lens down to f22 and maybe also change the ISO setting to 100 or 50 (see below).

Exposure compensation (Canon) / EV Exposure control (Nikon)

EV stands for exposure value. It refers to a system for manually adjusting exposures, compared to the settings that the camera meter gives you. It can be changed in steps of ½ or 1/3 stop but 1 stop changes are more normal for landscapes.

Use this function to compensate for overexposure or underexposure on single exposures. If your image is overexposed (the light areas have little detail) try -2 (minus 2) stops of adjustment. If you are in aperture priority the shutter speed will be changed by 2 stops (for example, the setting will go from 1/30 to 1/120 second). After making the changes take a picture and review the image obtained, with its histogram, and make further changes as needed.

Exposure bracketing

Many digital cameras can be programmed to take multiple images every time you press the button, each exposure separated by a pre-set amount. You can use this to make sure that when you take an image you are sure to have one that has the level of detail required in important areas of the image.

Turn it on and set it to take a total of 3 images, 1 or 2 stops apart. This is a really good way to understand the effect that changes in exposure have on the final image.

Digital camera sensors cannot cope with the brightness ranges that black and white negative film can. The way to get around this deficiency is to take the 3 images suggested above but with the camera firmly supported on a tripod. Each image will then be identical except for exposure. These can be merged together using Photoshop to give a final image that has detail in all areas. The technique is called High Dynamic Range (HDR) photography and articles on it can be found most months in at least one of the digital camera magazines.

Meter mode

Matrix metering (Nikon) and Evaluative metering (Canon) are now so good there is often no need to consider any other metering mode.

If you want to try something else the Spot metering mode (not on all cameras) is probably the one to use. Point it at mid-tones, or slightly brighter areas, in the scene being taken and compare to the matrix/evaluative reading to decide which to use. Check the exposure is good using the playback screen and the histogram function.

Getting the exposure right

If you make the effort at the time of taking the image you will then have everything you need to make good prints in image editing software such as Photoshop or Paint Shop, etc.

Use Aperture priority for most landscape photography.

Image too light (overexposed):
Increase the aperture by 1 stop from f11 to f16, or change the shutter speed, e.g. from 1/30 to 1/60.

Image too dark (underexposed):
Make changes in the opposite direction from f11 to f8, or 1/30 to 1/15.

Manual adjustment of single exposures: use the EV exposure compensation feature.

Automatic compensation for both over and under exposure: use the exposure bracketing function which will involve taking 3 images every time you press the shutter button.

White balance
Leaving this on Auto is fine for most situations and especially when first starting to use digital cameras. Once you understand the other camera settings then try changing this according to the lighting conditions. They are usually self-explanatory; sunny, cloudy, etc.

Cable Release and Self timer
Use a cable release to fire the shutter when using your camera on a tripod. This avoids any chance of camera shake when the shutter button is pressed. In the absence of a cable release the self timer function can be used instead.

Image checks after exposure

Playback screen: DISP (Canon) or (Canon & Nikon)
The playback screen is one of the most important parts of digital cameras because it allows you to instantly see your composition and exposure, something a film photographer had to wait days and weeks to see.

Image playback is usually done by pressing one or more buttons. Check out which ones do this for your camera. Sometimes pressing the same button several times scrolls round different views including image display with settings, image display showing clipping, histogram view and data view(s).

Become familiar with the playback screens as quickly as you can after acquiring any new digital camera. It is the gateway to most of the camera controls and image review functions.

Histogram
This is one of the most useful aids to tell you if your exposure was good or not. On most SLR cameras it can only be viewed after taking an image.

In general, we find images with large white areas without detail less acceptable than large dark areas with no detail. Sometimes we don't accept either which could be a problem! In order to retain detail in the lighter areas you must adjust the exposure. The playback screen is often not good enough to judge this so the histogram view should be used.

In simple terms, a big spike on the right represents light areas in your image (sky, snow, white water, etc) and if touching the right side of the graph indicates over exposure. A big spike on the left represents the dark areas in your image (shadows, etc) and indicates under exposure. Spikes in the middle represent the mid-tones in the image.

In images where the light areas are more important than the dark ones, exposing to produce a histogram with the spikes as far to the right side as possible, without touching the right axis, is best.

Highlight mode (Highlight – Nikon, Highlight alert – Canon)
This is one of the playback options on digital cameras. When turned on it will flash either black or red (depending on the camera) in overexposed areas where there is no detail, such as the sky or white water. If the flashing on playback of every image annoys you then turn it off and just use it on an ad hoc basis.

If you want to compensate for the loss of highlights (detail in the light areas) reduce the exposure by using a smaller aperture (like f22 instead of f16) or use a shorter exposure time (e.g. 1/60 instead of 1/30 second). If you are unable to do either of these, try increasing the ISO setting by 1 stop (e.g. from 100 to 200).

Composition

- 'Rule of thirds': This is probably the most useful guideline for photographers. It recommends that the photographer mentally divide the picture into 9 equally sized sections using 4 lines, rather like a noughts and crosses board. Some cameras can superimpose a grid on the screen to aid composition. Placing important elements on the lines or the points where they cross one another often makes them more pleasing to the eye. Use it as a guideline, it is not a rule and many fantastic images will not fit the grid!

87. Skiddaw from High Rigg
Skiddaw with snow on the tops from the summit of High Rigg, a small peak southeast of Keswick. A good demonstration of the 'Rule of Thirds'.

- People in landscapes: Some scenes work without people in them while others are improved by the scale that people give to an image. If you're not sure, try both and decide later. If included, an uneven number of people (1, 3 or 5) will give a more pleasing result than an even number but it very much depends on the arrangement of the people. Try and avoid an overlap of people in the shot or the result can appear confused or difficult to make out.

- The simpler the shot, the better it works: Don't cram lots of things into your images. Use your zoom lens, or change lens, to cover only what is important.

- Lead-ins: Use these to take the eye of the viewer from the lower part of the image to the centre of interest (but not so far that it leads out of the sides or the top; this can weaken a picture!). Examples include walls, streams or mountain ridges.

- Foreground interest: This can be something like a shapely rock or tree, grasses, a rucsac, in fact anything that adds to the rest of the image without overpowering it. Whatever you include in the foreground it needs to be in focus so pay attention to the depth of field settings that you are using.

- Check the edges of the image: Before you press the shutter button look around the edges of your composition for any distractions that you can remove by slightly changing your zoom, position or height at which you take the picture from. You may be surprised by how much you can improve an image just taking a few extra seconds to do this.

In Conclusion

These are simplified notes but, when used with a camera manual, they will guide you towards better pictures through understanding your camera more. Digital cameras have dozens of functions and settings; many do not concern landscape photographers. You don't have to learn everything in the manual!

Good luck, and if you need more help my final suggestion is that you come on one of my courses!

technical data

PLATE	TITLE	FORMAT	FILM	CAMERA	DATE TAKEN
foreword	Scout Scar view to the Coniston Range	7 x 6	Ilford FP4	Mamiya 7	5-Jun-09
introduction	Lingcove Falls in Winter	7 x 6	Ilford FP4	Mamiya 7	21-Jan-07
1	Blencathra from Castlerigg Stone Circle	7 x 6	Ilford FP4	Mamiya 7	9-Jun-08
2	Ashness Bridge	7 x 6	Ilford FP4	Mamiya 7	6-Mar-09
3	Blencathra from Castlerigg Stone Circle, Infra-red	7 x 6	Ilford SFX	Mamiya 7	9-Jun-08
4	Blencathra from High Rigg	7 x 6	Ilford FP4	Mamiya 7	6-Mar-09
5	Blencathra and Keswick	7 x 6	Ilford FP4	Mamiya 7	6-Mar-09
6	Blencathra Sharp Edge	35mm	Ilford FP4	Nikon FE	13-Oct-85
7	Winter Sun, Buttermere	6 x 6	Ilford FP4	Mamiya 6	19-Jan-01
8 (+front cover)	Buttermere and Fleetwith Pike #1	6 x 6	Ilford FP4	Mamiya 6	19-Jan-01
9	Buttermere Tree Reflections	6 x 6	Ilford FP4	Mamiya 6	19-Jan-01
10	Cat Bells and Derwent Water from Crow Park Keswick	7 x 6	Ilford FP4	Mamiya 7	6-Mar-09
11	Buttermere and Fleetwith Pike #3	7 x 6	Ilford FP4	Mamiya 7	8-Mar-09
12	Crummock Water and Mellbreak Reflections	6 x 6	Ilford FP4	Mamiya 6	14-Jan-01
13	Causey Pike and Grisedale Pike from Derwent Water	7 x 6	Ilford FP4	Mamiya 7	6-Mar-09
14	Dalt Wood Borrowdale	7 x 6	Ilford FP4	Mamiya 7	15-Apr-07
15	Grasmoor from Wandope	6 x 6	Ilford FP4	Mamiya 6	7-Sep-99
16	Derwent Water and Skiddaw from Surprise View	7 x 6	Ilford FP4	Mamiya 7	6-Mar-09
17	Cat Bells from Friars Crag	7 x 6	Ilford FP4	Mamiya 7	6-Mar-09
18	Buttermere Reflections and Fleetwith Pike	6 x 6	Ilford FP4	Mamiya 6	19-Jan-01
19	Sail, Ard Crags and Helvellyn from Wandope	6 x 6	Ilford FP4	Mamiya 6	7-Sep-99
20	Mellbreak and Crummock Water from Whiteside	6 x 6	Ilford SFX	Mamiya 6	7-Sep-99
21	Skiddaw, Bassenthwaite and Log	7 x 6	Ilford SFX	Mamiya 7	9-Jun-09
22	Skiddaw and Bassenthwaite	7 x 6	Ilford FP4	Mamiya 7	9-Jun-09
23	Skiddaw from Castlerigg Stone Circle	7 x 6	Ilford FP4	Mamiya 7	9-Jun-09
24	Skiddaw and Derwent Water	7 x 6	Ilford FP4	Mamiya 7	9-Jun-09
25 (+frontispiece)	Buttermere Icy Shoreline	6 x 6	Ilford FP4	Mamiya 6	19-Jan-01
26	Watendlath Tarn	7 x 6	Ilford FP4	Mamiya 7	6-Mar-09
27	Great Gable from Sprinkling Tarn	6 x 4.5	Ilford FP4	Mamiya 645	15-Dec-91
28	Great Gable and Scafell Range	6 x 6	Ilford FP4	Mamiya 6	23-Oct-00
29	Ennerdale Water from Red Pike	6 x 6	Ilford FP4	Mamiya 6	14-Jan-01
30	Yewbarrow, Great Gable and Wast Water	7 x 6	Ilford FP4	Mamiya 7	21-Jan-07
31	Bowfell and Crinkle Crags from Hard Knott	7 x 6	Ilford FP4	Mamiya 7	4-Jun-09
32	Ennerdale Water	7 x 6	Ilford FP4	Mamiya 7	8-Mar-09
33	Esk Falls #2	7 x 6	Ilford FP4	Mamiya 7	21-Jan-07
34	Coast near Eskmeals	7 x 6	Ilford FP4	Mamiya 7	5-Jun-09
35	Esk Falls #1	7 x 6	Ilford FP4	Mamiya 7	21-Jan-07
36	Devoke Water	7 x 6	Ilford FP4	Mamiya 7	4-Jun-09
37	Pavey Ark and Stickle Tarn	35mm	Ilford FP4	Nikon FE	26-Jan-85
38	Harrison Stickle	35mm	Ilford FP4	Nikon FE	26-Jan-85
39	Helvellyn Range from Harrison Stickle	35mm	Ilford FP4	Nikon FE	26-Jan-85
40	High Walberthwaite View	7 x 6	Ilford FP4	Mamiya 7	5-Jun-09

PLATE	TITLE	FORMAT	FILM	CAMERA	DATE TAKEN
41	Langdale Pikes from Elter Water	7 x 6	Ilford FP4	Mamiya 7	29-Sep-08
42	Scafell Pike	7 x 6	Ilford SFX	Mamiya 7	8-Jun-08
43	Ravenglass Boats	7 x 6	Ilford FP4	Mamiya 7	5-Jun-09
44	Scafell Pike from Wast Water	7 x 6	Ilford FP4	Mamiya 7	8-Jun-08
45	Lingcove Falls Reflections	7 x 6	Ilford FP4	Mamiya 7	8-Jun-08
46	Lingcove Falls	7 x 6	Ilford FP4	Mamiya 7	21-Jan-07
47	Scafell Range from Hard Knott	7 x 6	Ilford FP4	Mamiya 7	4-Jun-09
48 (+back cover)	Scales Force #1	6 x 6	Ilford FP4	Mamiya 6	5-Sep-99
49	Yewbarrow, Great Gable and Wast Water, infra-red	7 x 6	Ilford SFX	Mamiya 7	8-Jun-09
50	Wasdale Head Rapids	7 x 6	Ilford FP4	Mamiya 7	19-Jan-07
51	Scales Force #3	7 x 6	Ilford FP4	Mamiya 7	8-Mar-09
52	Seatallan Falls, Wasdale	6 x 6	Ilford FP4	Mamiya 6	7-May-05
53	Wasdale Head Falls	7 x 6	Ilford FP4	Mamiya 7	19-Jan-07
54	Scoat Fell View to Steeple and Ennerdale	6 x 6	Ilford FP4	Mamiya 6	16-Oct-99
55	Yewbarrow and Wast Water from Ill Gill Head	6 x 6	Ilford FP4	Mamiya 6	5-May-04
56	Rydal Water	7 x 6	Ilford FP4	Mamiya 7	27-Sep-08
57	Aira Force	7 x 6	Ilford FP4	Mamiya 7	7-Mar-09
58	Raven Barrow	7 x 6	Ilford FP4	Mamiya 7	7-Jun-09
59	Old Man of Coniston and Dow Crag	7 x 6	Ilford FP4	Mamiya 7	6-Jun-09
60	Old Man of Coniston and Tree	7 x 6	Ilford FP4	Mamiya 7	6-Jun-09
61	Helvellyn from Castlerigg Stone Circle, Infra-red	7 x 6	Ilford SFX	Mamiya 7	9-Jun-08
62	Helvellyn from Birkhouse Moor	35mm	Ilford FP4	Nikon FTn	16-Dec-84
63	Helvellyn from Ill Bell	7 x 6	Ilford FP4	Mamiya 7	28-Sep-08
64	Helvellyn from Castlerigg Stone Circle	7 x 6	Ilford FP4	Mamiya 7	9-Jun-08
65	Grasmere from Loughrigg Fell	7 x 6	Ilford FP4	Mamiya 7	27-Sep-08
66	Grasmere Reflections #1	7 x 6	Ilford FP4	Mamiya 7	27-Sep-08
67	Grasmere Reflections #2	7 x 6	Ilford FP4	Mamiya 7	27-Sep-08
68	Middle Tarn Old Jetty	7 x 6	Ilford FP4	Mamiya 7	7-Jun-09
69	Helvellyn from Striding Edge	35mm	Ilford FP4	Nikon FTn	16-Dec-84
70	High Street Sky	35mm	Ilford FP4	Nikon FE	8-Mar-86
71	Old Man of Coniston and Coniston Water	7 x 6	Ilford FP4	Mamiya 7	14-Apr-07
72	Rydal Water from Loughrigg Fell	7 x 6	Ilford FP4	Mamiya 7	27-Sep-08
73	Wise Ean Tawn, Sawrey	7 x 6	Ilford FP4	Mamiya 7	6-Jun-09
74	Striding Edge in Winter	35mm	Ilford FP4	Nikon FTn	16-Dec-84
75	Scout Scar Edge	7 x 6	Ilford FP4	Mamiya 7	29-Sep-08
76	Tarn Hows	6 x 4.5	Ilford FP4	Mamiya 645	16-Sep-90
77	Striding Edge and St Sunday Crag from Helvellyn	6 x 4.5	Ilford FP4	Mamiya 645	11-Oct-87
78	Small Water and Haweswater from Nan Bield Pass	7 x 6	Ilford FP4	Mamiya 7	28-Sep-08
79	Thirlmere from Helvellyn	6 x 4.5	Ilford FP4	Mamiya 645	11-Jan-87
80	Brant Fell View North	7 x 6	Ilford FP4	Mamiya 7	29-Sep-08
81	Windermere from the Langdales	35mm	Ilford FP4	Nikon FE	26-Jan-85
82	Windermere from High Street	35mm	Ilford FP4	Nikon FE	8-Mar-86
83	Windermere from Gummer How	7 x 6	Ilford FP4	Mamiya 7	7-Jun-09
84	Ullswater Trees	7 x 6	Ilford FP4	Mamiya 7	7-Mar-09
85	Winter Thaw, Raise Beck	6 x 4.5	Ilford FP4	Mamiya 645	11-Jan-87
86	Grasmoor and Crummock Water	6 x 6	Ilford FP4	Mamiya 6	16-Jan-01
87	Skiddaw from High Rigg	7 x 6	Ilford FP4	Mamiya 7	6-Mar-09